what's your excuse
for not living a life
you love

what's your excuse ...

 FOR NOT

LIVING A LIFE
YOU LOVE?

**Overcome your excuses and lead
a happier, more fulfilling life**

monica castenetto

"Monica has a reassuring and wise voice throughout … which lends support, succour and a sense of being in safe hands. This book gently urges you to find your path and realise the joy of being in your flow – when life, love and all that comes your way feels easier, more joyful and not something you need to resist with excuses.

Let this book guide you to fearlessly reap the gift that is rightfully yours – your life – and leave those excuses on the shelf along with unwanted fears and unfulfilled dreams"

Carole Ann Rice, Life Coach, Author and Daily Express columnist

"Whether you are thinking or dreaming of doing something different with your life, from giving up your corporate job and becoming self-employed to moving countries, or whether you are looking to make smaller positive changes to your life, this is the book for you! Down to earth and frankly awe-inspiring, it wants you to know that you can live a life you love.

Monica is one of the most fabulous and thought-provoking ladies I know and her book provides excellent advice and inspiration to get your creative juices flowing. Anything is possible in this life, and Monica is there to guide you, and help YOU reach YOUR goals and dreams"

Jane Hardy, Director of Fabulous Women and Marvellous Men

"This book truly reflects what Monica is great at – helping you to map out your change and get started with it, turning what seem to be challenges into manageable steps. Use it to create some structure for your change, and gently get beneath the surface of what is holding you back. Just like Monica's coaching, this book will never direct you; instead, it supports you in identifying your own solutions, with all the flexibility you need for the individual that you are. It's also really enjoyable – and I now feel more motivated and confident to achieve the changes I want to make in my life!"

Mark Rouvray, Activ Web Design

"Monica's enthusiasm for life, her energy for following her own varied interests and her grounded, supportive and well-structured coaching programmes stimulate and inspire her clients to find ways to live the life they love."

Nicci Bonfanti, Sales Coach and Mentor, Director of Manage2Improve and Trusted Sales Dynamics

"King Solomon in his wisdom spoke of seasons, and a time for every purpose. Change is inevitable and, as with the seasons, death is necessary for birth and growth. Monica Castenetto in her wisdom discusses in this book the so-many-ways that 21st century man

and woman get stuck in one season, not being able to make the transition to the next.

If we don't make the change ourselves, change will make us. So much better to take charge of uncovering, discovering or rediscovering our pioneering, risk-taking selves, and work towards living a different kind of life – a life that is ours. As Monica says, it's not about a perfect life, but about a life that is perfect for you. This easy to read yet profound book, full of practical wisdom, should be a gift to every young adult. We would create a world of happy, contented people!"

Andrea Encinas, Director of British Gospel Arts and Winner of Lady Hilary Groves *Making Music* Award

"Monica has written an extremely simple and useable book with many practical tips to help you succeed in living the life you love. Through her own personal journey, and through coaching her clients, Monica is aware of all our excuses and the little voice in our head which prevents us from moving forward, and she provides practical and helpful guidance about what to do when your mind is getting the better of you. I find Monica's book hugely motivational – it makes me feel like I have the support of a very trusty friend to hold my hand as I take my own steps towards living the life I love".

Erin Lewis, Yoga Teacher & Therapist

Also in this series

What's Your Excuse for not....

Getting Fit?
Eating Healthily?

What's Your Excuse for not Living a Life You Love?

This first edition published in 2016 by WYE Publishing
9 Evelyn Gardens, Richmond TW9 2PL
www.wyepublishing.com

ISBN 978-0-9933388-4-7

Cover and text design by Annette Peppis & Associates

Printed in UK by Marston Book Services Ltd, Oxfordshire

'What's Your Excuse…?' is a UK Registered Trade Mark
(Registration No: 3018995)

www.whatsyourexcuse.co.uk
Follow What's Your Excuse…? on Twitter – @whats_yr_excuse
https://www.facebook.com/whatsyourexcusebooks

www.livealifeyoulove.co.uk
Follow Monica on Twitter – @monicastenetto

Contents

Introduction

Stuck in a life you don't love?

Would you be happier if you changed your life?

But do you somehow remain stuck, and keep putting off making changes?

Perhaps you've reached a big birthday and even though you have what looks like a good life, you've now started to question whether it's meaningful enough and true to who you are. Or your marriage has ended, or your children have left home, and you're faced with the task of re-building life on your own. Or maybe you've been made redundant, or faced a health issue, or a life-changing decision?

There are many situations which require us to adjust our lives, and yet making real changes – even for the better – can be uncomfortable. And so we often find excuses to avoid doing it. And we stay put in a life we don't really like anymore.

Sound familiar? It does to me and in my experience letting our 'stuck' moments in life go on for too long will take its toll.

This book is here to help you avoid that.

What is a life you love?

I once did a survey of people who were interested in living life more fully. I asked them about their *single key ingredient* for a happy life.

(You might want to have a think about this yourself, before reading on.)

The top five key ingredients were:

* Love
* Happiness
* Freedom
* Loved ones
* Self-discovery

Money, in case you're wondering, came 9th, but a wide variety of ingredients were mentioned. You can read the full survey at www.livealifeyoulove.co.uk/research.

What the survey demonstrated to me is that everyone wants different things, so if *your* key ingredient is not among these five don't worry because a life you love will be completely individual and unique to you.

It might be focused on meaningful work, or centred around your family. It might revolve around your passion, or have spiritual notions at its heart. Or it might balance earning a living equally with making time for your loved ones, interests and yourself.

It might be paced at a rhythm that suits your nature – fast and furious, or calm and contemplative. Perhaps you love living mainly in the *external* world of people, things and actions. Or perhaps you prefer to travel in the *internal* world of thoughts, feelings, and reflections.

Or a little of all of the above.

What is it for you? Why not spend a little time reflecting on this – consider writing down your thoughts.

Finding, creating and living a life that feels truly ours is part of our purpose as human beings. As we become aware of our talents and qualities we can build a life which puts these to good use.

This gives us a sense of meaning, and makes us feel alive. And others will benefit from it too, which, in turn, satisfies us again. It's a virtuous circle!

There is no Perfect Life, only a life which is perfect *for you*. So you can exist *with* yourself, not *against* yourself. And live from a place of happiness and fulfilment, rather than from a place of fear, boredom or stress.

What a relief that would be, don't you think?

The benefits of living a life you love

Research shows that living a life which suits who we truly are has a positive effect on our wellbeing, even when it sets us apart from others[1]. This is true of both personal life and work.

For me, starting to live a life I loved took away the unease of being in a corporate career which just wasn't right for me anymore. Leaving that job freed up my energy to build the life I really wanted and I found an inner sense of purpose, happiness, alignment and connection with those around me – noticeable not just to myself but to others too.

Now, working as a life coach, I see this happen in my clients. They visualise a better life, shed the ties that bind them to their old life, and start moving towards the life they want to live instead. It's beautiful to watch – one of the great privileges of my work!

Spend a few moments now considering these three questions:

---

1   *Abigail A. Mengers, University of Pennsylvania: The Benefits of Being Yourself: An Examination of Authenticity, Uniqueness, and Well-Being, 8-1-2014*

- What makes you want to live a life you love?
- Why is this important for you?
- How will you feel when you're living it?

Jot down what living a life you love will mean to you. This is your personal *Benefits List*. If the going gets tough, use it to remind yourself why you are working towards a life you love.

If you're not sure, here are some ideas:

- I will live my life with a sense of purpose and fulfilment
- I will feel generally happy and satisfied. I will enjoy my life
- I will be motivated and able to achieve what I want in my life
- I will have a positive and optimistic outlook on life
- I will have energy and feel alive
- My connections with friends, family or partner will have improved
- I will be more resilient through life's inevitable ups and downs
- I will make more purposeful choices
- My confidence and self-esteem will have grown
- I will feel my life matters

The cost of *not* living a life you love

Staying in a situation that is not right for us anymore is stressful, unsatisfying, and will eventually cost us dearly. Our confidence and courage will be eroded and our ability to make the changes we need to make will diminish. We will then end up feeling increasingly powerless and despondent. At the very worst we may end up hating our lives and feeling cynical and pessimistic.

In short, staying stuck in a life that isn't right for us will sap the life force right out of us!

Don't wait until this happens to you. If you change nothing, nothing will change. So take an honest look at where you stand, and how you're feeling about your life.

Creating change in your life

Creating a better life means *changing*. That is, moving away from what doesn't serve you any longer and bringing things into your life which suit you better.

This may just involve a few tweaks – going part-time at work, arranging to work from home one day a week, buying your vegetables from the local market instead of a big supermarket, or changing your fitness routine.

Or it may mean a more significant change – moving to another country, breaking up from a long-standing partner, or retraining for a new career.

If you've ever tried to bring about a change in your life (small or large) you may appreciate that it's not always easy.

> There will be times when you're inspired, motivated and excited

There will be times when you're inspired, motivated and excited by the new opportunities your change brings. Things then seem to flow effortlessly and almost by themselves.

But inevitably, there will also be times when you

don't know what to do, or where to go. When you feel small and scared about the risks your change involves; when you worry about the loss of status, money or a relationship. When you don't dare do what you really want to do, because of what others might say, or when you face resistance from others. Or when an old habit has you in its grip and you just cannot ditch it.

Then there's change itself. No matter how positive it may be, it can also be uncomfortable, as it naturally involves endings and uncertainty. In order to open a new chapter in our lives we often have to close a previous one. We must bear the uncertainty of not knowing what's going to happen next, and get used to unfamiliar territory. And we must risk moving forward even though we will never be able to know exactly what the future may bring.

We're faced with all of this when we're imagining, planning, or working towards a life we love. It tests our purpose, vision, and staying power, so no wonder we have a natural resistance to change!

Before we know it, we find ourselves backing off and using excuses – "it's easier to stay where I am; my current life isn't so bad after all; I can probably make it work if I just learn to cope with the stress; so many people in this world are *not* living a life they love – isn't it presumptuous of me to assume that I can?"

This book has been written to help you overcome all

of your excuses and to find a way of making the changes you need to make.

A word about excuses

There are always reasons why *not* to do something, and some of them will be valid. You really may have no money to buy the home you want. You really may have no clue about what you want in life. You really may lose your income if you leave your stressful job.

Yet what matters is that you don't use these as excuses for not getting on with the things that really matter to you.

> Our excuses are a protection we hide behind

You know you're making excuses when you're using them to avoid something which is important and much-needed in your life. Our excuses are a protection we hide behind. They're our shield against things we're scared to try. But excuses diminish our confidence in dealing with the challenges life throws at us. In her book "Choosing Happiness" Stephanie Dowrick even maintains that they sap our self-respect[2]. So we don't want to stay in that place for too long!

Just because our fears of change are real, doesn't

---

2   *Stephanie Dowrick, Choosing Happiness, Allen & Unwin Australia, 1 Jan 2005*

mean we can't work through them. In fact, overcoming them, and taking a risk is a must in order to achieve some of the most important and worthwhile stuff in our lives – finding work we truly love, committing to a partner, caring for others, starting a family, achieving a breakthrough in our field of expertise, creating a business, making the world a better place. Whatever is important and worthwhile to you.

It's by taking risks that we get beyond our fears and really experience life. It's how we grow and develop as people. It's how we become wiser, more tolerant and more compassionate. It's how we build our self-confidence.

So don't let excuses stand in the way of *your* important, worthwhile stuff! *You* know what that stuff is. Be honest with yourself. Jot down some of the excuses you are making right now to avoid changing your life for the better. You will find ways of addressing them in this book.

How this book will help you

This book is *not* another coaching book on performance and achievement. It won't suggest that you should be striving to be more than you are. It won't suggest that you should be constantly striving to be bigger, better, more successful, higher-achieving, better-performing, richer or more important. And it's not a boot-camp programme to whip your life into perfect shape either.

Instead, it's here to help you overcome your excuses, so that you can make the changes required to create a life which is right for you. It is intended to help you keep going through your difficult moments – because you may not be too far from a breakthrough.

Your life will continue to have its ups and downs. Things will continue to go well and not so well for you. And constantly chasing a vision of a perfect life is only going to make you feel inadequate. So this book is also intended to assure you that you are *enough*, and that all you need is already inside you. You just have to draw that out. The more you do that, the better you will deal with any tough times.

This book will provide you with the resources, support and encouragement you need to change your life. Read it from cover to cover, and let it fill you with motivation, or use it as a quick reference guide, to get you through those tricky moments when you feel discouraged, and when an excuse might easily get the better of you. Just look up that excuse, and read the tips on how to tackle what's going on for you at that moment.

You can make the changes required to create a life which is right for you

Then set aside your excuses and keep going – happiness might just be around the corner!

If you find yourself coming up with innovative and creative excuses which did not appear in this book or if you want to share how this book has helped you, please email me at monica@livealifeyoulove.co.uk. I would love to hear from you, and may incorporate your experiences into the next edition of this book!

The Excuses

Readiness

When we've reached a point where we're really ready to change, we usually make it happen.

So what's readiness all about?

Well, it's a tipping point. You might reach that point when you get so dissatisfied and frustrated with your life that you just can't bear it any longer – when an honest comment from a friend shakes you up, or when you realise that how you live doesn't help you or makes others suffer. But there are positive tipping points too – when you've researched your plan sufficiently and feel completely prepared to go for it; when your enthusiasm for a change gives you wings; or when you get inspired by someone else living in a way you'd love.

The key point here is that change starts on the inside. Change in our *external* life which is visible to others is usually the result of a prior *internal* shift.

"Change is a process, not an event," says psychologist James Prochaska[3], who has extensively researched, written and taught about this. Looking for the secrets of successful personal change, he and his colleagues interviewed thousands of people who had positively and permanently altered their lives and he discovered that

---

3   *James O Prochaska, John C Norcross, Carlo C DiClemente,*
Changing for Good, Harper Collins, 1994

change does not depend on luck or willpower. Instead, it's a six-stage process.

It starts when we acknowledge that we have an issue and need to do something about it. We then become aware that change is possible, and start weighing up the pros and cons. Eventually we make a decision and start preparing. And *then* we take action. Finally, we look at maintaining what we have achieved.

Until we've reached that point of being ready on the inside, change in our outside life is unlikely to happen, even if we try to force it.

So we don't need to beat ourselves up anymore for not immediately springing into action when we want a change, because our first step forward may not necessarily be an action. Sometimes, it's actually about something happening *internally*.

Read on to find out how you can overcome what feels like a lack of readiness.

I'm not ready

What exactly are you not ready for?

In my experience, when we say this, we often mean we're not ready to take action. We might feel we need to ponder our situation a bit longer. We might not know exactly what we want, and be waiting for inspiration. Or we might feel that taking action would be premature for all sorts of reasons.

That's OK. We all go through our process of getting ready on the inside to create change visible on the outside.

But beware of staying stuck there! If you feel that happening to you, here are some questions to help you get mentally prepared to make your change happen:

- How able are you to admit that you don't love your life, or have an issue that needs addressing? Who could you talk to about this?
- What would a positive change look like for you?
- How strong is your belief that a change is possible, and that you can do it? What could strengthen your belief?
- What do you need to let go of before being able to move forward in your life? What decisions do you need to make?

If you fancy doing a bit more work on this, check out my free quiz How Ready Are You For Change In Your Life? at http://livealifeyoulove.co.uk/how-ready-are-you.

If you don't know what you want, see "I don't know what I want".

Now is not the right time

When I worked as a consultant in the corporate world, I would joke over dinner with colleagues about whether there was a life beyond consulting. Much as our work was stimulating and rewarding, we were also feeling the strain of it. Yet it seemed impossible to contemplate doing something else. It didn't help that the work was so full-on that none of us had any time or mind space to research other options. There was always something urgent to do, or a new challenge to take on. It never seemed the right time for change.

It's easy to overdo 'waiting for the right moment'

This meant that I stayed put for a few years longer than I might have otherwise. Even when I was thinking about changing my career, I never quite found my way to actually handing in my notice, until my company got taken over and I just couldn't reconcile the changes this brought to my work. And that's what, eventually, made me take the long-needed action and leave. Sometimes the best helping hand is a good, firm push!

It's easy to overdo 'waiting for the right moment', and slide into fear, doubt and indecision. The more we put off action, the more our change starts to look bigger, riskier and scarier than it is. And the easier it becomes to feel that now is not the right time.

Therefore consider giving yourself that good, firm push, or setting yourself up to receive one – in the best possible way. It can work wonders! Alternatively, try setting yourself a deadline for the change you want, and organise it so that by then you'll just *have* to do it.

If this idea worries you, try to remember a change that was sprung onto you by circumstance in the past, whether you felt the time was right or not. And uncomfortable as it might have been, notice how you still managed to pull through – and possibly go on to better things.

A friend's story is a great example of this. In her job with a prestigious company she felt, in her own words, "Like an ant under somebody's shoe" and her mental and physical health were suffering. Yet she stayed, not ready to leave the security of her regular salary. Eventually she was driven out by unacceptable changes within the company. At first, she felt frightened, insecure and worried about the future. Yet looking back, she can now see how this change forced her to take a successful plunge into self-employment. Today, she uses her expertise much more productively, spends more time with her family, and is happier, healthier, and more confident than ever before.

It's never the right time for change. So how about

that old saying of pulling a rotten tooth sooner rather than later? Just get on with it – and make *now* the right time.

It's not all that bad, after all

We tend to say this when we get scared about making a change, or when making a change has become discouragingly difficult.

Suddenly, it seems much more appealing to stay where we are, and make our unhappy circumstances work. A friend of mine calls this staying with the 'half-happinesses and almost-satisfactions'. That could be staying in a job you don't like because it pays well, or staying in a relationship that doesn't work because it feels better than the prospect of being alone.

Now, sometimes, learning to love the life you're living *is* the solution. The change then happens in how you see things. For example, for a long time one of my clients thought that she wanted to stop working in business and turn her passion for the environment, which she had been pursuing in her spare time, into a new profession. That was until she realised that she actually preferred keeping work and passion separate. And what she really needed to do to be happier was to stay in her job, but update the way she engaged with her passion.

If you're hiding from a necessary change and telling yourself that your life isn't so bad after all, ask yourself these questions:

- What is the cost of avoiding this change – to your happiness, your health and wellbeing, your loved-ones?
- And what are the benefits of making the change you're putting off? Remind yourself with your personal Benefits List

Now are things really not so bad? Do you really want to stay where you are?

It's not my fault

What isn't? Being stuck in a life you don't love? Not doing anything to change it? Or both?

Maybe it's because your parents didn't love you enough, you have suffered a trauma, your self-esteem is low, or society and other people are putting spokes in your wheel.

I appreciate these are obstacles, and they do cause

us pain. We all face some difficulties in the course of a lifetime.

But try not to fault-find or blame. It's not about what others 'do to you'. Others will always be others. And the world will always be the world. Let them be so, and do *your* thing.

This is about the life *you* will love to live

This is about the life *you* will love to live. And, if you're not living it at the moment, it's about what *you* can do about that. Ultimately, that is the only power you have.

So grab that power!

And ask yourself how blaming others helps? And if you realise that it doesn't help, what could be a more helpful attitude?

Whatever others may have done or said, being in a life you don't love doesn't make you a bad person. It's just where you happen to be now. It's only from there that you can start to change something.

What one small thing in your life can you change today? Start with that. Do it now.

I haven't got enough information

Doing research and analysis to understand things better is a key stage of personal change. It's how we work out how to make change happen in the real world.

However, if we go on and on with it, we can be struck by *analysis paralysis* – confused by all the data we find, we can't see the wood for the trees any more. We become uncertain of what we want, and unsure of whether we want it at all. And we end up stuck!

So how much information do you really need at this stage?

The truth is you'll never be able to know everything in advance. And the information you do have might be incomplete, or even contradictory.

> We can be struck by *analysis paralysis*

The good news is that you don't have to have it all perfectly worked out to get started.

So know when enough is enough. Then step back from your research.

What conclusions can you draw from what you have? What is still unknown, but impossible to find out now? And which first steps can you undertake right now?

Do those. Get underway. And trust that what you don't know now will become clearer as things progress!

I can't decide

How do you normally make your decisions?

Think of a decision in your past which you made successfully. What did you do, and how? And how could you use that approach to help you make the decision you're facing today?

Still can't decide? OK, so if you secretly knew what was best for you and were totally honest with yourself what would you decide?

Finally, if that hasn't helped, here's a fun way to unstick your brain. Answer these questions, quite quickly, without thinking about them too much:

- What would happen if I decided X?
- What would happen if I didn't decide X?
- What wouldn't happen if I decided X?
- What wouldn't happen if I didn't decide X?

Now what have you discovered?

Mind

This is the chapter of toos, nots and can'ts. It's about that insidious little voice inside us which keeps suggesting that change is too hard, not possible, can't be done. If we keep listening to it, we end up believing it.

The trick is to know that this little voice is not speaking the truth. It is informed by judgments and stories from your past experience, or from observing and interpreting what happens around you. Bad stuff of course happens to all of us, but so does good stuff. It's just that because of our survival instincts we register the bad stuff much more strongly than the good stuff. And our impressionable little voice hooks onto the bad, losing sight of the good. It speaks of our fears and insecurities.

So when you find yourself using the words 'too', 'not' or 'can't' in a statement about yourself, challenge it. Put it in proper perspective. Is it really true? All the time? How do you know? In which other ways could you see this?

Finally, if someone else uses these words when speaking to you about the changes you are making in your life, then remember George Bernard Shaw's insight that "the people who say it cannot be done should not interrupt those who are doing it" and just keep going.

Read on for more about changing your mind set.

It's too big

Improving your life needn't necessarily be a huge undertaking.

Small tweaks can make a huge difference – leaving your office on time every day, shopping somewhere different, accepting compliments instead of deflecting them, or scheduling in more quality time with family and friends.

What small tweak would make a difference to *your* life?

Of course other changes can indeed be bigger, for example quitting your job for something better, moving abroad or leaving a toxic relationship.

The best way to tackle a big change is to treat it as a project and break it down into manageable steps. List everything that needs to happen. What needs to happen sooner, what later, and what depends on what? Make a rough plan, and display it somewhere visible.

Small tweaks can make a huge difference

Then you can make a start with the most immediate actions, and work your way forward gradually – a little bit each day or week, sometimes more, sometimes less. And keep it flexible. If something doesn't work as you hoped think about how you can do it differently? How do you need to change your plan?

When working on something big, you can easily feel that you're not making much progress and will never get to where you want to be.

So here are a few tips for staying motivated:

- Record your completed actions. Tick them off on your plan, with big, fat ticks in your favourite co-lour, if you like. Ticking things off is a great reward for our brain and will make you feel good about your change.
- Review your progress regularly. Remind yourself of where you first started, then look at where you are now. When we're immersed in the daily minutiae of our change we don't recognise how much we've actually already progressed!
- Celebrate and reward yourself. Award yourself a gold star when you reach a significant point or complete something difficult. Allow yourself a treat, take a break, or celebrate with a friend.
- Have a supporting structure. To keep going on your own can be hard, no matter how motivated you are. So arrange for regular meetings with a friend or a coach. Share ideas with like-minded people. Find someone supportive to witness your work, share your struggle and acknowledge your progress.
- Tackle issues promptly. Issues will inevitably arise, so don't let them fester, hoping they'll go away by

themselves. Name them, think about what might resolve them, or ask for advice. The sooner you do it, the better for your progress, your energy and your motivation.

For an inspirational story, see "It takes too long".

I'm too old

Today, more and more people are living to be a hundred. That's a lot more life than people had even just a century ago! Why not make the most of that extra time by spending it on meaningful pursuits?

Many of my clients are in their forties and fifties. They've lived a while, been through ups and downs, and know themselves better now. They've done the rat-race, want to start looking beyond it and to build a life that feels truly right for them. They want to savour life and not rush through it, live purposefully, do something meaningful and give back.

I have clients in their sixties too. They see retirement looming, and yes, they want to slow down. Yet they feel they're too young for a comfortable armchair existence, hidden away from the world. They still have a contribution to make.

The world is full of examples of people re-inventing themselves in later life. Activist Maggie Kuhn founded the Gray Panthers movement when forced into retirement at 65. She said that older people constitute America's biggest untapped and undervalued human energy source. Holocaust survivor Frieda Lefeber started painting at 76, earned her Fine Arts Certificate at 83, and celebrated her 100th birthday with her first solo art exhibition in 2015.

Closer to home, London entrepreneur Trisha Cusden was in her sixties when she founded a business of pro-age make-up products, to celebrate the beauty of older women rather than fretting about the wrinkles. And a good friend of mine was well into her fifties when she 'upped sticks' from Germany, and moved to London with her husband (who was in his seventies) to start a new job at an international publishing company. A year later, she was made redundant and successfully switched to freelancing in the same industry.

I myself gained a professional qualification in Contemporary Dance at the Trinity Laban Conservatoire when I was 36 – one of the best things I

The fact is you're likely to be around for a whole lot longer!

ever did in my life. 97% of my fellow students were at least ten years younger than me, but one of them was

72 years old – and he was a sought-after, international performer!

You might be feeling too old, but the fact is you're likely to be around for a whole lot longer! The responsibility for how you spend that time is yours. Granted, we're not all meant to be activists, entrepreneurs, and brilliantly talented artists. Nor are we all meant to make huge, sweeping changes to our lives. But if you're fed up with your life, it's only ever too late to make changes for the better if *you* decide it is.

It's too late

Even if you don't feel too old, you might still feel that you have left it too long and have now missed the boat, or have made a mistake from which you cannot recover.

But is this really true? Ask yourself:

* What if you could start afresh at any time in your life?
* What if you could catch that boat? Or catch the next one? Or another one altogether?
* And what if you could make amends for your mistake? Or simply forgive yourself and move on?

Here's Richard Bach's test (from his book Illusions) to find out whether your mission on earth is finished – "If you're alive, it isn't."[4]

At the end of our lives we'll probably regret more what we *didn't* do than what we did. As Caroline Myss says, "Do you really want to look back on your life and see how wonderful it could have been, had you not been afraid to live it?"[5]

Sure, sometimes we leave things a bit late, or make seemingly irrecoverable mistakes. Sometimes life gets in the way. But your dreams don't have a shelf-life. And if one route ends in a cul-de-sac, you can always look for another route and try again – for as long as you're alive!

See also "I'm too old".

I haven't got the confidence

Confidence isn't something you either have or don't have. Rather, it's a quality you acquire by *doing* things.

Action breeds confidence and courage, so the more you do things you're nervous about – speaking in

4   Richard Bach, Illusions: The Adventures of a Reluctant Messiah, Dell Publishing Co, 1977
5   http://addictquotes.blogspot.co.uk/2010/08/empowering-quotes-by-caroline-myss.html

public, getting back in the dating game, or going to job interviews – the more your confidence will grow.

It doesn't even matter whether what you do is 100% successful or not. Experiencing success will obviously boost your confidence, but even an unsuccessful attempt will be helpful – you could feel good about simply having been courageous enough to try. You might realise that 'failing' is not so terrible after all. You could well feel encouraged to try again – and do better next time. All of that will boost your confidence.

> The first steps are the hardest. It gets easier after that

So start taking action and confidence will come. The first steps are the hardest. It gets easier after that.

Three tips to ease you into it:

* Start small and build up gradually. For instance, if you need to speak in public, have some one-to-one training, practice on your own, then speak to one friend, or two, or three. Then try it with a friendly, small audience. Then with a larger audience. Only move up to the next bigger challenge when you've built up your confidence with the smaller ones.

* Practise and prepare. Using public speaking again as an example, practice your presentation skills and rehearse your talk. Write it down if necessary. Imag-

ine yourself giving your talk successfully. Have your notes to hand. Plan what you're going to wear. Visit the venue you'll be speaking at. Make sure you're 'fed and watered' in good time before you speak. Do whatever helps you feel more able to take on your challenge.

* Get support. Who can help you – particularly with those difficult first steps? Who can give you tips and advice? Hold your hand? Encourage you from the sidelines? Pick you up if you fall? Whether it's a family member, friend, coach or mentor, you don't have to struggle on your own. Ask for help. Be open to receive it. And be surprised at what happens.

As you take these actions, enjoy feeling your confidence grow.

See also "I don't have the courage".

I can't do it

Listen to what you're saying to yourself or others. Does this sound like you?

* I can't leave this job even though it's not right for me

- I can't possibly register on a dating website to find a partner
- I can't take time off to travel and find out what I really want in my life

Ann Brashares writes, "The problem is not the problem. The problem is your attitude about the problem."[6]

Statements containing "I can't..." are very limiting

Statements containing "I can't..." are very limiting. They shut down all possibilities from the start. If we repeat them too often, we will start believing them. And before we know it, they become our 'normal' way of thinking.

So notice when you think or say "I can't" and ask yourself where does that statement come from? Is it really true? All of the time?

I would venture to say that, if you chose to leave your unloved job, no one could really stop you. If you decided to get on that dating site, you would be able to do so. And if you really made up your mind to go travelling, you would find a way of making it happen.

You can always choose your attitude – so just for a moment, allow yourself to think, what if I *could* do these things? And if you really can't do these exact

---

6   Ann Brashares, *The Sisterhood of the Travelling Pants*, Delacorte Press, 2001

things, then which other things *can* you do, that will move you closer?

That little voice saying "I can't" may be the loudest one in your head right now. But you can choose to acknowledge this, challenge it, and put another voice in its place which says, "Actually, I can..." Then listen to that.

Allow yourself to think, what if I could do these things?

By turning your can'ts into cans, you turn your dreams into plans.

I haven't got what it takes

A variation of the previous excuse, this is your belief that somehow you're not good enough to make a life change happen.

I have a talented friend who wants to write a blog, but doesn't, because she doesn't believe that she is capable of writing articles which people will want to read.

If something similar is holding you back – if you believe that you're not tough, determined, smart, talented or organised enough to change your life – ask yourself where this belief came from.

Did someone say something to you in the past

which made you believe this? It might have been a parent, or a teacher – someone in authority whom you believed when you were a child. But think about it *now*, as the *adult* you are *today*. Were they really right?

If my friend decided to write whatever she *can* write, I very much doubt that not a single person in the world would read it! And if her concern is about not getting enough readers, how will she know without trying? How could she appreciate that reader numbers are something to build up over time, rather than an instant measure of success or failure?

Now, if you're worried that your skills might not be up there with the most stellar talents in the world they can still be good enough for now. What if you could just start using the skills you have today, and improve them along the way? What would you do then?

As poet Henry van Dyke said, "Use whatever talents you possess. The woods would be very silent if no birds sang there, except those who sang best."

Give it a try and see what happens.

It hasn't worked before

Why bother again, you wonder. Well, past failure does not preclude future success. Rather, it's a great learning opportunity – you can begin again, but more wisely.

So how do you do that?

Firstly, don't keep doing the same thing again and again. If you always do what you've always done, you'll always get what you've always got. It will feel like bashing your head against a brick wall.

Past failure does not preclude future success

Then, *reflect* on what you've done in the past. What worked and what didn't? What can you learn from this and, most importantly, what do you need to do differently next time?

Though ridiculed, Thomas Edison made over 10,000 attempts to invent the light bulb. Finally, in 1879, he demonstrated the world's first light bulb which glowed well, was long-lasting and was affordable. Asked by a reporter, "How did it feel to fail 10,000 times?" Edison simply replied, "I didn't fail 10,000 times. Mine was an invention with 10,000 steps".

Modify your approach, and find something that will work

Edison's invention was achieved by extensive trial and error. He kept going because he believed that what he wanted to achieve was important and worthwhile.

Can you see your life change as a trial and error process too, and keep going until you find *your* breakthrough? If something didn't work in the past and needs to be abandoned, learn from it. Modify your approach, and find something that *will* work.

I'm a creature of habit

Yes. All human beings are.

Habits are deeply ingrained in us. They form when we repeat something again and again, until we do it automatically. They help us function effectively, without having to think about it. But they also make it difficult to do things differently and often they are the very things we need to change in order to improve our life!

Set realistic expectations

Say you decided to eat more healthily. For a little while, it goes well. But then your old chocolate habit is still more powerful than your new fruit eating habit and you slip back to eating chocolate again.

An established habit feels like putting on an old, perfectly fitting glove, whereas a new habit will (for a while) feel like a glove that hasn't quite been broken in yet – stiff and uncomfortable. No wonder we abandon new habits so easily and slip back into old ones!

One of the keys to successfully introducing a new

habit lies in repeating it for long enough – wearing that new, uncomfortable glove until it fits you perfectly. Your brain will build new pathways, so your new habit becomes your normal way of doing things.

One study found that this takes 66 days *on average*. They also found this varied greatly, anywhere between 18 and 254 days, depending on whom they studied, and which new habit they chose to introduce![7]

Therefore, set realistic expectations. Kicking an old, unhelpful habit and introducing a new, more useful one is not going to be a quick fix. Yet it's not impossible, it just takes time.

The science of habit change could probably fill an entire library, but here are a few pointers to get you started:

● Treat your habit change as a process which will happen over time, not an event. Whether it takes you 18 or 254 days, you'll get there. Forget about the number, start with Day 1, and keep going.
● Don't just try to eliminate bad habits, replace them instead. If your nail biting habit relieves stress or boredom, find something else to do that for you

7   *Phillippa Lally*, Cornelia H. M. van Jaarsveld, Henry W. W. Potts and Jane Wardle: "How are habits formed: Modelling habit formation in the real world"; European Journal of Social Psychology Volume 40, Issue 6, pages 998–1009, October 2010; http:// onlinelibrary.wiley.com/doi/10.1002/ejsp.674/abstract*

instead. You could chew gum, or have a snack. Just be sure to have it to hand when stress or boredom strikes.

- Make your new habit as simple as possible. Make it so easy that you can't say no. For instance, to reduce your sugar intake, start by putting a quarter of a spoon less sugar in your coffee each day – until that feels normal. Then reduce it by another quarter spoonful and get used to that, and so on, until you're where you want to be.

- Support your habit change with a system. A client of mine became a regular runner by laying out his kit in the evening, so it was the first thing he saw when he got up in the morning – reminding him to go for that run. He made his run as easy as possible, and built it up over time. And afterwards, he rewarded himself with a nice cup of tea. If you put a system like this in place, in time, your brain will look forward to the reward and help you do the task in order to earn it.

The good news is that falling off a new habit horse every once in a while doesn't affect long-term successful habit formation – as long as we keep getting back on the horse. So keep at it – one day at a time!

It's self-indulgent and selfish

"So many people don't live happy lives. Why should *I* deserve it? How selfish, to think about *my* happiness when others are unhappy. And the poor people in the third world – they're struggling with *real* problems, like not having food or clean water, or surviving wars. Living a life I love sounds trivial compared to that – a total luxury, really!"

If these are your thoughts, ask yourself how staying in a life you hate is affecting your energy, mood, health and well-being? And how it's helping other people?

Living a life you love is not a hedonistic pursuit, nor is it removed from reality and the problems of this world. It too answers an important human need – the need to become truly and fully you, and to accomplish everything you can[8]. It helps us feel fulfilled and at peace with ourselves, even when our life circumstances are difficult and it is from this place that we can start truly giving back to and helping others.

Hence, I would say that working towards a life you love is not a luxury, but a necessity – particularly in Western societies where we are experiencing a decrease in social cohesion, where many people are earning lonely livings in stressful jobs that disconnect them from

8   Read more about this in Abraham Maslow's, *The Hierarchy of Needs – A Theory of Human Motivation, 1943*

their true selves and where these things have a negative effect on our health.

So go ahead. Live a life you love. Live your life as you wish. You owe it to the world.

Fear

Moving towards a better life inevitably involves change.

For instance, if you are stuck in a job you hate chances are you won't love your life any more by staying put and suffering in silence. You may need to be more assertive in meetings, speak to your boss about a pay rise, stand up to an office bully, or leave that job and find one that suits you better.

Simple, right? Well not really.

Because what often holds us back from doing these things is fear. Fear comes up in different shapes and forms in most of my coaching conversations. And I would be lying if I said I've never felt it myself.

So what are we afraid of?

In the above examples, you might fear that your colleagues will react negatively to your new assertiveness, or your boss might laugh at your request for a pay rise. The bullying might get worse, or you might not find another job and lose your financial security.

Those are valid reasons to be afraid. Yet they're not the whole story. For starters, we don't know if what we fear will actually come true. It might not!

And we may even be fearful of aspects of positive change – the sadness about leaving colleagues behind, the uncertainty about whether you'll be successful in a new job, or the effort involved in learning to do things differently. [9]

But one thing is certain. Change in our life is inevitable. So how about, instead of labelling it 'good' or 'bad', just seeing it as *change*, with both its joys and discomforts?

Because we *can* get over our fears. By tapping into our courage, facing our fears, and doing the very things we're afraid of. It gets easier every time we do this. We'll see that what we fear is just a paper tiger. And we'll get stronger, more confident and more courageous each time we face our fears and triumph over them.

It's too risky

Let's say you want to leave the job that's been making you miserable, or learn to speak up in meetings, or invite that person you've been admiring from afar to dinner. But it's too risky, so you don't do it.

What are you *really* afraid of? Ending up unem-

---

9   *Social scientists have found a way of measuring this. In an article titled "The Social Readjustment Rating Scale", T.H. Holmes and R.H. Rahe document the stress level of all kinds of life changes*

ployed if you leave your job? Your colleagues responding unpleasantly if you speak up? Or feeling embarrassed if the person you invite out says no?

How can you know that these things will happen? What other things could happen instead?

Try putting things in proper perspective. What is the worst that *could* happen? And if that did happen, so what? You might well find that actually it wouldn't be so terrible. After all, nobody would have died – and you'll get over it!

> Try putting things in proper perspective

Still scared? Then maybe take inspiration from people with jobs where somebody actually *might* die if the worst happens. Say, brain surgeons, stunt people or extreme mountaineers. They go to great lengths to plan, check and re-check during their preparation, and have safety procedures and contingency plans in place. They minimise the risks wherever they can, then get on with their jobs. Having your own safety procedures in place might, in some cases, help you – rehearse an awkward conversation in advance or check out the object of your affection's favourite restaurants in advance of asking them out.

The fact is though we can't predict the future. Therefore every change contains an element of uncertainty. Even if we plan and prepare well it's impossible to predict *exactly* how things are going to pan out, but many of the most worthwhile things in life require us to be able to take a (measured) risk. So remind yourself of the benefits your change will bring. Aren't they worth the risk?

See also "I don't have the courage".

I don't have the courage

I want to invite you to sit back and relax. Remind yourself of a time in your adult life when you had to do something you were afraid of, and you faced your fear and did it anyway. Can you remember:

- What it was that you had to do?
- What you were afraid of?
- How it felt – your fear, your doing it regardless, and looking back after you'd done it?
- What you did to move past your fear? How did you do it?

So where can you find that same courage now? That's where you've got to go again.

Courage is a place of deep knowledge that something needs to be done, and that waiting will only make our fears worse. It's where we surrender all of our 'ifs' and 'buts', face our fears and just get on with it. And it's a consequence of having learnt that we can get through these things, and feel better afterwards!

Now, if you can't find any examples of past courage, start cultivating courage in your life today. Ask yourself what you're afraid of. Then ask yourself what act of courage, however small, could you undertake *right now,* in order to face that fear, and move one step closer to a life you love?

Remember also that "Courage doesn't always roar. Sometimes courage is the quiet voice at the end of the day, saying: I will try again tomorrow."[10]

What if I get it wrong?

I hear this a lot. Many of my clients are afraid of taking the wrong path, of making the mistake of changing their life only to find that they're not happy in their new life either, or of missing something better altogether. Is this you?

Then let me ask you, how can you know what is 'right' or 'wrong' for you? And what's so terrible about going 'wrong'?

---

10   *Mary Anne Radmacher in her book Courage Doesn't Always Roar, Conari Press, 2009*

I worked with a client once, an interim manager, who was determined to become CEO of a charity. She really got stuck into it, doing the necessary research and leveraging her contacts. It was not until she started applying for a CEO position that she realised she actually didn't want it at all! Reflecting on this, she discovered that her desire to be a CEO had been all about proving a point, and not about the role itself. She recognised that the responsibilities of a CEO would put her in a strait jacket. She actually loved variety and, being a 'creative fixer', was much happier with the work she already had – where she could make a real difference to a client, and then move on to the next.

So had this lady wasted her time, made a mistake, or been somehow embarrassed by going down the 'wrong' path? No! There is no 'right' or 'wrong' way for you to create a life you love; only *your* way. It's not done by thinking up the perfect plan, executing it perfectly, and seeing any deviation as a mistake. My client learnt

> Set your direction of travel, take your first step, get started

something important about herself, got her long-standing CEO wish out of her system, and turned her energy to other life changes; that is, she made a positive step towards a life she loves.

The experiences *you'll* have as *you* move towards a life you love might well change you, your views and your plans. You might only know if something is not for you after you've tried it. So don't expect your progression to happen in a neat, straight line.

Don't worry about getting it 'wrong'. Set your direction of travel, take your first step, get started. But be prepared to adjust your course along the way!

I don't want to be a failure

This excuse is linked to the previous one – only, it's about judgment.

So you've had this vision of a life you love. To be a charity CEO, to be a better partner, to travel the world, start a business, write a book; you've given it your best efforts, and somehow, it didn't work out as anticipated – you didn't make it.

But who says this means you're a failure? Other people? Or maybe yourself?

You cannot, of course, influence what others are going to think or say. But you *can* influence how *you* think about what's happened (and you may want to reconsider being around other people who put a negative spin on things).

So you didn't get the result you wanted. How does this matter? What if it was possible to think of this as just something that's happened, without labelling it as 'success' or 'failure'? And what can you learn from it?

You are where you are. What do you want to do about *that*? Do you want to let your vision go, because you now understand that it wasn't right for you in the first place? Or will you persevere, and find another way? Focus on that, and let others think what they will!

See also "What if I get it wrong?"

I don't want to be disappointed

Sometimes things won't turn out as you hope. A relationship you work to improve still breaks up, you've got a great new job but need to step back due to illness, or you get made redundant.

No matter how positive your mental attitude, you're likely to feel disappointed. It's a risk we must take when we embark on changing our lives – after all, not everything is in our control. The trick is not letting this stop us.

What helps here is not to be too fixed in your views of what you want – a general direction of travel will often do. Know that unforeseen things can happen along the way, and that you might not come out where you hoped to. Anticipate that you will have disappointments, but remember that you will get over them. If you need proof, remind yourself of other disappointments you've had in your life – and note how you've recovered from them.

Then go for your change, with enthusiasm and passion, and give it your all!

See also "I don't want to be a failure" and "It's too risky"

I'm afraid of getting lost

Changing your life can indeed be disorientating. As we start letting go of our old life, things can and do get a little chaotic.

In change management theory, there's an idea of creating change by unfreezing the old ways as if they were a block of ice, making a change when everything is in a fluid, melted state, and then re-freezing things in the new, improved way.

Leadership advisor Robin Sharma sums it up: "Change is hard at first, messy in the middle, and gorgeous at the end."[11] Chaos is inherent in big change.

---

11 http://www.robinsharma.com/blog/10/my-20-best-quotes-for-high-achievement/

It looks like that melted messiness in the middle is where we can get lost. Yet it's also an inherent part of every change. So be prepared for a somewhat bumpy journey, to lose sight of the horizon for a while, and possibly for things to get worse before they get better.

Can you find a part of you that is OK with that? A part of you that knows things aren't always clear-cut, which is happy to sail that fluid, melted sea, until new, more solid shores appear? A part of you that trusts that, eventually, things will become clear again?

Do you have things or people in your life to support you and help you find your way, in uncertain times? A loving partner, a trusted friend or travelling companions? And can you have a strong enough vision of the life you're aiming at to carry you through your change when it gets messy? Then you've got your recipe for overcoming this excuse!

I don't want to look stupid

"You're telling me there's no perfect way to change my life," I hear you say. "And that adjusting my course, living with trial and error, going round in circles or making U-turns is OK. But if I really start doing this, others will think I've completely lost it!"

This, too, is about judgment – see "I don't want to be a failure" which applies here, too!

I'm afraid of taking responsibility

What is it that makes this scary?

I recently read an example of how the ancient Romans applied the principles of personal accountability. Any engineer who built a bridge had to stand underneath it when the scaffolding was removed, whilst an army marched over it. My research hasn't revealed a reliable source for this, so it might well be a myth. Still, it's a great metaphor for having the courage to hold yourself to account for your actions.

Now, we won't get crushed by a bridge if we make a mistake on the way to creating a life we love. But accepting accountability for it can still feel difficult – particularly, if our change affects others too.

> But if *you* aren't responsible for your own destiny, then who or what is?

But if *you* aren't responsible for your own destiny, then who or what is? Other people? Circumstances?

It's certainly easier for us to *blame* them – particularly when things are not going well. That way, we don't have to feel bad about the consequences of our own poorer, not-so-wise choices and actions.

But here's the thing. Accountability is not about blaming yourself. It's about saying, "This is what's going on in my life, and it's because of what *I've* chosen to do, or because of how *I've* chosen to respond to what happened to me. If I don't want that, then *I* can do something different, or respond in a different way." It's about taking ownership of your life with all that works and all that doesn't. It's about being able to take full credit for what worked, and being willing to make repairs for, or moving on from, what didn't.

> Others respect us more for being accountable – and love us more for being human

Owning your destiny in this way might be uncomfortable when you first start, but it gives you back what you've given away – the power to choose the life *you* want to live. It will free you from being the victim of what others, or circumstances, 'do' to you. And it will make your life feel really *yours*, warts and all.

Accepting and owning our mistakes can be very liberating. Admitting to being fallible relieves us of the pressure of having to be perfect. It gets us out of the 'blame game', and we can stop feeling defensive. And we can deal with guilt by taking action to make good what we may have done wrong.

It's also true to say that others respect us more for being accountable – and love us more for being human.

In essence your life and your destiny is *yours*. Make a decision now to own it. The reward, according to author Brene Brown? "If you own this story, you get to write the ending."[12]

For thoughts on dealing with mistakes see "What if I get it wrong?"

I'm afraid of success

This sounds strange. Yet many of us sabotage our own chances of success.

Do you have this fear?

It might be because you feel you don't deserve to be great. You might ask, "Who am I to be wonderful, rich, talented, successful, and generally living a life I love?" Or you might associate being successful with feeling uncomfortable due to others' competitiveness, judgment or envy.

---

12   http://brenebrown.com/2015/06/18/own-our-history-change-the-story/

In some cultures, being successful is misunderstood for boasting or showing off – just observe if your environment encourages excessive humility or self-deprecation. You might worry about losing friends if you become too successful, and you might worry that you'll become unlovable, if you are seen as powerful enough to live a life you love – women in particular tend to be concerned about this.

However, how does making yourself smaller than you are to prevent others feeling insecure, judgmental or envious help the world?

I'm not suggesting that you aim to be the greatest person who ever lived. I'm suggesting that you nurture and demonstrate the specific greatness that is within *you*. The world, in order to be better, needs all of us to do this, and to make a difference in our own way, however small. You can make a difference not only to yourself, but to others too.

Now, this involves *owning* your real self, your weirdness, your weaknesses and shortcomings, and also your beauty, your uniqueness, your exceptional skill, your human warmth, and your greatness. And yes, it takes courage.

Practise celebrating your own greatness from now on – whether it's your character, personality, skill, humanity, or your capacity to enjoy life. Here are some starting points:

- Set aside self-deprecation, cynicism and excessive humility
- Start accepting compliments with a smile and a thank you. Don't deflect the compliment onto others and don't attempt to make an achievement sound smaller than it is. Equally, no self-aggrandising. Just own what you've done well and say thank you. Full stop
- Think about what it is that you're really great at. If you gave this more expression, how would it help the world? And how would it help you?
- Vow publicly (to family or friends) to utilise your talents, for the benefit of yourself and for others
- Where can you apply your strengths and talents in the world in a way which works for you? What small and easy thing can you start with? When will you do it? Reflect on this, record it in a journal, or discuss it with a person you trust.

A final, liberating thought from author Marianne Williamson: "As we all let our own light shine, we ... give other people permission to do the same. As we ... liberate ourselves from our own fear, ... we automatically liberate others."[13]

Empowering stuff!

See also, "It's self-indulgent and selfish"

---

13   *Marianne Williamson, A Return to Love, Harper Collins, 1992*

Time

In modern Western society time is at a premium. Most of us are constantly balancing our own needs with the complex demands of work, family, friends or hobbies. Information exchange is faster than ever before. We communicate across time zones, always available via social media and gadgets, and everything we ever want to know can be found – and vies for our time and attention – on the internet. A 2011 study by the University of California estimated that we are bombarded with the equivalent of 174 newspapers of data every day![14]

As a result of this, many of us are going through life feeling overwhelmed, being constantly distracted and finding no time for the things which are most important to us.

It's easy to put off finding time to create change in our life, even if that change is much needed. We reckon we can't possibly fit it in, on top of everything else we've got going on already. But what could be more important than spending time reflecting on the life you want to live, and doing what needs to be done in order to live it, making your time here on earth count and making a difference to yourself, others, and the world?

14   1http://www.telegraph.co.uk/news/science/science-news/8316534/
Welcome-to-the-information-age-174-newspapers-a-day.html

I haven't got the time

Time is a finite resource. We all have 24 hours a day, and a certain number of years of life. How we spend that time is, ultimately, our own choice and responsibility.

What could you stop doing, or do less of?

So I'm with Kevin Ngo, who says in his book Let's Do This, "If you don't *make* the time to work on creating the life you *want*, you'll eventually going to be forced to spend a lot of time dealing with a life you *don't want*."[15]

If you don't want that, take a good look at how you're filling your 24 hours each day. What are you giving your time to that is:

- a must have, and absolutely essential for your survival and comfort?
- a nice to have, but not absolutely necessary?
- a pure indulgence, or even unnecessary (if you're really honest)?

What could you stop doing, or do less of, in order to *make* the time to work on your life? Confide this to a

---

15   Kevin Ngo, *Let's Do This: 100 Motivational Messages to Inspire Action*, CreateSpace, 2013

trusted friend or a coach, tell them when you'll start, and promise to let them know when you've done it.

A client I worked with managed this extremely well. A busy marketing manager, she wanted to change her job, find a partner and spend more time abroad, but never found the time to make these changes.

Analysing how she spent her time allowed her to identify where she was wasting it unnecessarily and she was soon able to claim it back for what she wanted to do. She became more disciplined in leaving the office on time and stopped letting work distract her from other priorities in her life. She reduced time on social media, TV and lengthy phone calls and set aside specific evenings to work on what she wanted to bring into her life.

She dedicated time to dating, and within a year she met her new partner (and now husband). Happily he is from the Mediterranean which has enabled her to reconnect with languages and travel. Today she is working part-time for her old company and has launched a small business with her husband.

Could you find a similar path to reclaiming some time?

I'll do it later

"Now is not the right time to change my life," you say. "I'll do it tomorrow, next year, when my health gets better, when the kids move out, when I retire..."

Sure, there are times in life when there is a lot going on, and initiating a major change on top of it would be too much.

But tell me, how long have you been saying that you want to change your life, but telling yourself 'later'? And how many excuses have you found for 'later'?

If you answered 'ages' and 'lots', then do you really want this change that you keep postponing? Be honest!

Not really? Then let it go and stop talking about it. It will free you from the constant presence of an unticked box, making you feel guilty and a failure.

But if you really do want it? Then dig a little deeper. Why are you putting it off? What are you afraid of? Are you ready for this change? Do you know where to start? Read through the other sections of this book for help in answering these questions.

If you conclude that it's actually just a matter of getting over a bit of inertia, try one of these simple tricks:

* Raise your motivation. Think about all the good stuff that will happen when you make the change you want – see your personal Benefits List. Imagine

how wonderful you will feel hearing positive feed-back about your change. Promise yourself a reward when you've done what you want to do.

* Raise your sense of urgency. Remind yourself why your change is important now. If you need to, scare yourself into action by considering the possible consequences of not doing anything, then when you've made your change you can feel the relief of knowing that these things haven't happened.

* Put on a bit of pressure. Make a big announcement to your friends, your boss, or your colleagues, that you will do what you want to do. Also tell them by when. Do it in a way that won't allow you to wriggle out of it, even if it's just to avoid the embarrass-ment of not living up to your announcement.

My final tip comes from my clients who often refer to developing a 'Just Do It' mind set.

The time might never be right. So what if now was as good a time as any?

It will take too long

I have a friend whose life hit rock bottom some time ago. His industry had changed dramatically when a recession hit, creating huge losses in his business. His children were born with a disability that was not easily identified. His wife was desperately struggling to understand their needs, and became increasingly unhappy in her job. He was working day and night to save the business and support his family. He was sinking deeper into debt and lost the family home. His marriage was under serious strain. He knew he needed to make drastic changes, or lose all that was dear to him.

So he and his wife sat down together.

They put on the table all that wasn't going well. They created a new vision for where they wanted to be, in all aspects of their life. They hatched a plan for how that was going to happen, and stuck it on their kitchen wall. They made tough decisions: Closing the ailing business. Getting jobs. Becoming experts in the condition of their children, and finding the right support for them. Looking after their own health. Reviving their relationship.

They worked on their plan and their mind set every day.

It took them 3 years to clear their debt. During that time they started two new businesses which today are very successful and support their family. Having come through this massive life change together has transformed them personally and strengthened them as a couple. And their family life is rich and happy.

So yes, changing your life *can* take time. But how long is 'too long'?

The change *you* need may not be as drastic and transformational as my friend's. Then again, it might be. What matters, surely, is not how long it will take but *why* you need to make it, and what you and your life will be like when you've made it.

Bear in mind that a change that seems like it might take a while might *look* daunting.

Break it down into bite-sized pieces

However, if you break it down into bite-sized pieces, and work on them over time, it will *feel* much more manageable. You will get a sense of achievement from the smaller changes you put in place along the way. And things will gradually get better too.

How's that for a change of perspective?

See also "It's too big".

Money

There's hardly a change you can make which doesn't have a financial implication. For example, getting fit, even if you avoid a gym membership, might mean buying at least some pieces of clothing or equipment. De-cluttering your home might mean paying for the disposal of unwanted items. And these are only small changes. Bigger changes like leaving your job or moving to another country naturally carry bigger financial implications. Inspirational writers and speakers always encourage us to dream big and go for what we really love. Jump, they tell us, and the net will appear. Yet I find that the big question for almost everyone is, "How am I going to make my plan work financially?"

Well, if I had an easy answer to that, I'd be a millionaire! But what I *can* say is that whilst the money question is a very valid one, it can be overcome. "Empty pockets never held anyone back. Only empty heads and empty hearts can do that," says Norman Vincent Peale in his book "Enthusiasm Makes the Difference".[16]

Read on for my thoughts on why a perceived lack of money doesn't have to prevent you from making life changes.

---

16   *Norman Vincent Peale, Enthusiasm Makes the Difference First Fireside, 2003*

I can't afford it

Let's examine whether that's true.

A client of mine had been very successful in a varied and rewarding corporate career spanning two decades. Then his work started to feel increasingly repetitive to him, with no avenues for further growth.

Too young to stay put until retirement, he started to explore other options. The ones which really excited him were completely different working models to the one he knew. They involved becoming self-employed, or taking out a franchise.

Naturally, he wondered what not receiving his regular salary at the end of the month would mean to him. And he reckoned there would be an income gap, too, whilst he built up a new business.

His first response was to say that he couldn't afford it. But when he questioned whether this was really so, he found that, actually, he had put enough money aside in the past to carry him through a transition phase, even with no earnings at all. This eventually freed him to quit his job, and start investigating franchise businesses.

My client is by no means on his own. The more uncertain the change we are contemplating, and the more uncertain our future income, the more we will feel that we can't really afford it.

If this is you, here's a reality check:

- How much money will you need to make your change? Include things you'll need to buy, as well as getting through a time of low or no income.
- If you're taking a break from work, when can you anticipate money coming in again, and from where?
- Now look at the money you have. What savings or other sources of income do you have?

You may now feel that you can afford your change. Great news! Now you can move on.

But if the money you need really isn't there, read on.

I will lose my income

If your change involves leaving a job, then yes, you will. Or rather, you'll lose your income from *that* job. But that is not to say that you'll lose all income forever. And equally it's not to say that you cannot find ways, even temporarily, to sustain yourself whilst you're making your change.

Not all of us have enough money set aside to take us through a career or life change. And you know what? That's OK. Because there are many ways to fund a change. How creative can you be? How flexible? And how much uncertainty are you prepared to live with?

Some people find part-time, flexible, or interim work. A client I worked with, for example, ingeniously managed to negotiate an arrangement that allowed her to do most of her work part-time from home – so she was able to mitigate the stress of that work, still earn an income, and explore projects for her future.

Other people are very clever about setting up business-es and projects that secure public or private funding. Or they borrow what they need until they earn money from a new situation. Others again are fortunate in having a part-ner who is happy to sustain them during their change.

Are you able to find temporary or part-time work, or identify another source of funding?

See also "I don't want to be poor", "I don't want to lose my lifestyle" and "I'll lose my Frequent Flyer card".

Doing what I love doesn't pay

This is a tough one. Because in our society some jobs do command high incomes while others don't.

And yet, I believe that people rarely truly succeed unless they enjoy what they do. And Wayne Dyer says, "Doing what you love is the cornerstone of having abundance in your life".[17]

17   See http://www.brainyquote.com/quotes/quotes/w/waynedyer173497.html

One of my clients started out at a good girls' school with confident friends but she didn't do very well academically. This was not for lack of intelligence. Rather, she was uninterested in the curriculum, and unmotivated to apply herself beyond the minimum needed to get through. It was not until she went to art school to actively pursue her love of colours, patterns and fabrics that she started doing really well. She was loving her work and having fun with it. Like most artists, she did her stints with interesting, but low-paid work engagements – and then recognised that making a living from her work was important to her. Today, she is a successful fabric designer, dividing her time between an art director role at a well-known fabrics company and her own business, designing and creating fashion handbags.

> Love and passion ultimately don't care how they're lived out, just that they are lived out

A friend of mine, a talented painter, was always told that art was too unstable for her to be able to make a living and persuaded to take retail jobs instead. She did so, to fit in and get by, but ended up feeling at a dead end, tired and underappreciated. Eventually she realised that painting was the thing that made her happy, and changed her life to reflect that. She is now a self-employed fine artist, and although she still has a retail job to help pay the bills, she considers painting to be her *main* career, and views her retail work as her other, second job.

These are just two examples. Things are never perfect. Yet it seems to me that love and passion ultimately don't care how they're lived out, just that they *are* lived out.

I don't want to be poor

What does 'poor' mean to you?

I've been quite experimental and adventurous in changing my own life. I've had times of focused work, times of learning new skills, and times of exploring my options. I've had times of being healthy and fit, and times of living with serious illness. I've had times of sharing my life with others, and times of working things out on my own. As part of all that, I've had times of high income, low income and no income. The importance of money shifted depending on what else was going on in my life. And it still does.

There are two points to be made about my own experiences:

- The word 'times'. None of these phases in my life lasted forever. All of them, eventually, passed. Including the times of low income.
- I've never been 'having-nothing-to-eat-living-on-the-streets' poor (and I don't mean to judge anyone here).

So if you're not making your important life change because you're worried it will leave you in poverty, take a look at your current spending:

- What is absolutely necessary?
- What provides a bit of cushioning?
- And what, though nice to have, could you quite easily do without – at least for a while?

Be honest and really question your choices.

I know from experience that, once you start your change, you might well find that, actually, you don't really need all the money you thought you needed in order to feel secure and happy.

If you're still worried, ask yourself what would be the worst situation you could possibly land in? What or who could help you prevent this? And what could you do if your change didn't work out the way you hoped? There's nothing wrong with having a Plan B!

If you realise that what you're really worried about

is not so much being poor, but rather losing your life-style, see the next chapter.

I don't want to lose my lifestyle

How do you know this will happen? Is this really the case? And what exactly will you lose?

If you do find that your change will impact your life, what's more important, your current lifestyle or your dreams?

Remind yourself of the benefits of making your life change. Consult your Benefits List. Is maintaining your lifestyle more important than those?

If the answer is yes, which parts of your lifestyle are you *not* prepared to give up? Your home, your car, freedom to manage your own time? And which ones could you compromise on? Your holidays abroad? Regular wardrobe updates?

Now, how could you make your change, so that you maintain the most important parts of your lifestyle, and put the others on hold until you've made it?

And if your lifestyle is less important than you thought, you can start making your changes today!

A final word about this – if you do have to forego some of the luxuries in your life whilst making an important change, don't be disheartened. Keep reminding yourself that this is only one phase in your life, and it too will pass.

I'll lose my Frequent Flyer card

I empathise with this one – I'll admit that, after I left my consulting career, I really felt the sting when the blue card arrived, instead of the golden one I'd had before!

This sounds like a trivial excuse for not changing your life. Yet it can be an issue for many of us, because what it's really about is our feeling of status. Platinum cards convey importance and preferential treatment; so do powerful job titles, and the substantial pay cheques attached to them.

Losing these is not comfortable. You will ask yourself, who am I without the important title, the jetting around the world, and the preferential treatment?

And yet can you imagine how it will be good to experience being nothing but yourself for a while? And to learn to stand just as tall as you did as the holder of that Platinum Card? It could be a profound experience.

If you're not living a life you love because you're worried about losing status, ask yourself what does status mean to you? Is it about power and responsibility,

or respect, recognition and admiration? From whom?
What if your sense of power, responsibility and worth
wasn't dependent on titles or other people's admiration, but came from *you* – and was present, whatever your circumstances? What kind of a life would you
move into then?

See also "I don't want to lose my lifestyle".

Knowledge

As a rule, humans prefer certainty to uncertainty. Studies have shown that people would rather *definitely* get an electric shock now than *maybe* be shocked later, and show greater nervousness when waiting for an unpredictable shock than an expected one.[18]

Our brains like creating certainty, because this allows them to run on patterns, thereby saving energy and resources. Uncertainty, on the other hand, feels to our brains like a threat to our lives. Even just a little ambiguity can make us feel uncomfortable. And larger uncertainties, like not knowing whether your job is secure, can be highly debilitating.

So if you know you need to make changes in your life, yet don't know what or how, that can feel very stressful. Never mind not knowing how the changes will pan out!

This might result in you preferring the unhappiness of a life you hate (because at least you are certain of what it is), to a life change and the associated uncertainty of how you'll get there.

But this needn't be the case. Because if you start

---

18   Badia, P., McBane, B., Suter, S.: *Preference behavior in an immediate versus variably delayed shock situation with and without a warning signal. Journal of Experimental Psychology, Vol 72(6), Dec 1966, 847-852*

to explore, clarify and plan what you want for your life you'll reduce your feelings of uncertainty – and increase your level of comfort around change. Read on for tips, tools and tricks on how to do that.

I don't know what I want

The question 'What do I want?' will come up again and again for you at different stages of your life.

If you're thinking about it now, give that question time and space. Because it's hard to find inspiration about what's next in your life, when your time and headspace are filled with stress and dissatisfaction.

If you can, take some time off. Go somewhere quiet, or somewhere different. A client of mine has given herself a year to travel the world and do that. But if you can't go away, book time in your diary each week to work on finding your answers.

If you can, take some time off

You could search *out there* – observe what others in your situation do. Speak to people about it. Get inspiration from books or films. And notice how you feel about what you find.

Or you could search *within yourself* – what really

matters to you? What makes you tick? What have you had enough of, and what do you long for more of? Really get to know yourself, and draw ideas for what's next from that.

If this doesn't help, it might be easier for you to start by stating what you *don't want* anymore. Write it down, then flip it on its head: What's the opposite of it? Is this what you *do want* instead? Which other ideas come to mind now?

What makes you tick?

Go with your interests, and with what you're curious about. Explore and experiment. Try things on for size. Notice how they feel and go with what feels right (or light, as a friend of mine likes to say). Can you see how this might be rather fun?

Then, every so often, stop and ask yourself what you've learnt. Because, ultimately, your own inner wisdom is your best compass!

I don't know how

Well, all you need, really, is a rough direction of travel for where you want to go, an initial plan, and your first steps. And the emphasis here is on the word 'rough'.

You don't need to have all the answers up front, nor

work it all out in detail. Because chances are that things will change along the way, anyway. You'll learn from your experience. Unexpected stuff happens. And your views and priorities might change as a result of this.

So get started, and expect to adjust your course as you get further into your change. That way, you'll arrive somewhere that *is* right for you, instead of somewhere that *seemed* right in the beginning, but isn't anymore, because you carried on regardless.

You could, of course, work with a coach, who will help you find clarity, purpose, focus and accountability. He or she will provide a supportive and critical ear, tools and a structured process to help you along. If you like the sound of this, you can find more information on my *6 Step Process to Transform Your Life* here: http://livealifeyoulove.co.uk/6-steps.

See also "What if I get it wrong?"

I don't know where to start

Let me tell you a secret about this. In my experience, it actually doesn't matter *where* you start. What matters is that you *do* start.

By all means plan your change as much as possible. Use your logic *and* your gut feeling. If what you want looks overwhelmingly big, break it down into small steps. Look at what needs to happen first, and what can happen next or last. Prepare for your change, and have a Plan B.

What matters is that you do start

But then start *doing.* Do whatever is possible for you now because action builds confidence and prolonged inaction builds doubts.

To help propel you into action, you could start with what looks easiest, quickest, or simply the most fun.

In my coaching work I often guide my clients to do just that, particularly if they're a bit nervous. From all of the options they *could* choose, I ask them to pick the one that's easiest and then help them to plan it, so they know exactly what they need to do, and when and how.

You could start with what looks easiest, quickest, or simply the most fun

And nine times out of ten they come to their next session not only having completed their first easy step, but also having tackled some of the other steps they thought were going to be more difficult. Taking action gave them confidence, and they were on a roll.

Any journey begins with a single step, and no first step is too small.

If you're still not sure, ask yourself what simple

thing could you do this week that would move you *one step* closer towards where you want to be? Do that. And next week, do the next thing, then the next thing, and the next thing ...

I don't know how to explain it to others

So you're leaving your corporate career to go travelling, or to become a baker of additive-free breads. Or you're marrying a younger man and moving abroad with him. Or you're adopting a child as a single parent. Telling others about your life change can feel daunting – particularly if you expect that they will be puzzled or judgmental about your choices.

But not everyone needs to know the whole, detailed story.

So draw a circle and write in it the names of those who are closest to you. Then draw a wider circle around that, and write in it the name of your friends. In the next, even wider circle, write the names of colleagues, then acquaintances, and so on. The further out, the less close to you the people are.

Only those closest to you need to know the full, personal story. If they want to, that is. And if explaining your choices to them is important to you. The further out a person features in your circles, the less you need to tell them.

Now, what are you comfortable with telling the people in each circle? Prepare one version of your story for each. Write

Not everyone needs to know the whole, detailed story

it down, if necessary, and know how you'll answer likely questions.

Remember that this is *your* change, and *you* choose what you let people know about it. What they will think about your move, is *their* business, not yours.

See also "People will judge me".

Other People

"It takes courage to do what you want. Other people have a lot of plans for you." I think writer Joseph Campbell was right there![19]

Your parents might want you to get an education, whereas you feel you're the practical, get-going-with-a-job kind of person. Your friends might see the person you're dating as totally right for you, when you don't, or vice versa. And your community might expect you to settle down with a spouse, two children, a nine-to-five job and a dog, when you feel more like bouncing around as a free spirit. This is not to say that what others want for you is necessarily bad or wrong. Indeed, they often only wish the very best for you, and are genuinely passing on their life experience and wisdom. However, what they say also represents *their* view of what a good life constitutes, not *yours*.

What *you* are here for is to live *your* life

What *you* are here for is to live *your* life, with *your* view of happiness, *your* dreams and ambitions, *your* decisions, *your* experience, *your* measures of success, *your* learning.

---

19   *http://academyofideas.com/2013/12/joseph-campbell-other-people-have-a-lot-of-plans-for-you/*

"When you dance to your own rhythm, people may not understand you; they may even hate you," says author Sue Fitzmaurice. "But mostly, they'll wish they had the courage to do the same."[20]

So develop *your* courage and listen to yourself. Put that unique *you-ness* into the world. Listen to others' advice, but then live *your* life. Be OK with the fact that others might have a view about it. And remember that, actually, they might not!

Be who you are and say what you feel, because those who mind don't matter, and those who matter don't mind.

Others will see the real me

We all wear so many masks.

We do it to fit the roles we play with other people – parent, teacher, leader, tough girl, loyal employee, funny guy. We do it because it makes our interactions with others work and because we want to be accepted. Also, playing (or hiding in?) a role can give us a sense of safety.

I myself played out the role of high achiever for a

---

20   https://www.facebook.com/SueFitzmauriceAuthor

long time. This is a part of me, of course. But I also had another part in me which longed for a different life, a part which was creative and free, which wanted to take risks, experiment, live flexibly and pursue passions. A part which wanted me to utilise my talents and pursue all of my interests.

Needless to say, when I worked in management consulting, I never let colleagues or clients see that other part. I felt they wouldn't understand, and feared their judgment. In order to fit into that high-powered world, I thought, I needed to be driven, results-oriented, and business-like. And so I was.

Letting our *real, full* selves be seen puts us in a vulnerable place, yet it is also one of the most affirming things we can do.

If we step outside of the roles in which others have come to see us, we don't know what will happen. What if the truth of who we are is not acceptable to others? What if they turn away from us? Understandably, this can put us off creating a life that expresses all of our parts – including those weird and wonderful ones that make us uniquely us. This is about giving important aspects of your personality full expression, even when they are not necessarily 'mainstream'.

You don't have to make a big, dramatic gesture, like quitting your job, selling all of your possessions or buying a boat to sail around the world, and you don't have to make a big announcement to everyone (though you can, of course). Because slowly and bit-by-bit does it, too. Take your time to think about how *you* want to live your life. Embrace where that's different to what others might expect. Start with small changes leading in the direction you want. Decide what you feel comfortable telling people, or not – and start by telling a few people who won't judge you. (They won't necessarily be your family!) Then gradually expand from there. Also, remember that not everyone needs to know everything. Do it at your pace – but do it.

Once I started giving more expression to the creative part of me, my life opened up like a flower – and I loved it much more! And interestingly, the responses I'd feared actually didn't happen at all. Most of my business colleagues responded to my life changes with open minds and genuine interest. And I even discovered that some of them, too, had a hidden side to which they wanted to give more space!

> Allowing others to see the real you is an important step

Allowing others to see the real you is an important step that will strengthen and liberate you. Tap into your courage and reveal something of your real self – gradually, if you need to. And recognise that much of what scares you might just be in your own mind!

See also "I don't have the courage" and "I don't know how to explain it to others".

What I really want to do is weird

According to screenwriter and filmmaker Joss Whedon, "whatever makes you weird, is probably your greatest asset."[21]

What is 'normal', anyway? Wouldn't the world be a sad place if we all strove to be some kind of averaged-out, bland, mass-produced version of normal?

My Italian dad used to say, "Il mondo è bello perché è vario." The world is beautiful because it's varied.

Joline Godfrey says, "Weird is the fingerprint of your soul. Embrace it!"[22]

And I say, who you are and what you really want to do, however weird, is your unique contribution to the world. And the world needs it – to help us see things differently, and learn and progress.

> What is 'normal', anyway?

---

21   http://news.impossible.com/joss-whedon-the-man-who-brought-you-buzz-and-buffy-giving-you-free-screenwriting-class/
22   http://www.supercoach.com/tvdetail.php?recordID=142

Know that some people might well think of you as weird, but they will also get over and get used to it. And you might also find and indeed attract people who'll support, appreciate and enjoy your unique thing. I've often heard celebrity life coach Carole Ann Rice advise, "Send out your vibe and find your tribe!"

What will it take for you to *own* your weirdness, see it as interesting and different, and just get on with what you want to do in your life?

See also "People will judge me" and "Others will see the real me".

People will judge me

Yes. Sadly, some people might well do that.

But they are likely to judge you whatever you do, whether you stay in the life you hate, or move into a life you love. Whether you stay employed, start a business, or quit work to go travelling. Whether you marry, live with your partner, start a family, or stay single. And whether your hobbies are walking and gardening, or breeding rare South Sea turtles.

Much as we long to be accepted and liked by everyone, there will always be people who make negative judgments.

Understand that people's judgment of you is *their* problem, not yours. Directing their negative feelings onto you is their way of making themselves feel better, when *they're* stuck and unhappy in their own life.

What you have to do is keep your eyes on *your* path, *your* life, *your* change. As I read recently, "Ignore the boos – they usually come from the cheap seats." And focus on those people around you who are positive and supportive.

> Focus on those people around you who are positive and supportive

Also read "I don't want to be a failure", and "I don't want to look stupid".

I'll lose my partner / family / friends

Changing your life may well have an impact on the people in your life. But how can you know how it will affect your relationships?

Perhaps you're worried that what you want is very different to what you have right now with your loved ones, or that they won't be willing or able to follow you where you want to go.

Have you talked to them about it? Until you do, you won't know how they feel. When you share trust, mutual understanding and support with people, it should be possible to talk about your life goals with them. Be sure to explain why the change you want is important to you. And also be open to exploring how it can sit with the life you currently have with them – or how you can build a *joint* vision for your future life together.

I coach many clients who have a partner or family. Some of them have come up with new life visions for themselves, which involve big changes such as long travels, retraining and going back to work after a family break, or even moving abroad and start-

Talk to your loved ones

ing a new business. I've yet to meet the client whose relationship or family split up as a result of bringing about what *they* wanted to do next in life!

Having said that, there's no guarantee that this won't happen to you. Perhaps you'll hit a deal-breaker – say, you really want children and your partner really doesn't. Or you find you need distance from someone who has been in your life for a long time. Or a friend cannot be part of the life you envisage, and chooses to leave.

Most change, even when positive, brings with it some kind of ending – something or someone we leave behind, in order to move forward with our life. In the case of people we love, this truth is hard to accept. However, not everyone is meant to be with us forever – nor are we always meant to be with them. So when it's time to let someone go, can you do so, and be grateful for all they've given you? Not easy, but sometimes necessary.

Denying yourself a life you love for fear of a relationship coming to an end will take its toll. So honour *your* life path, create *your* vision, and take a risk. Talk to your loved ones about it, and see what happens. And whatever happens – you'll still have the choice of how to respond to it.

My kids need me

"How old are your kids?" I asked the lovely lady who contributed this excuse. "Oh, they're in their twenties, and independent!" she replied, and burst into a peal of laughter. She knew she was making excuses!

Now if you have very young children, this might not apply to you, as young children do indeed need a lot of your time and energy, but if you're using obligations to other adults as an excuse, ask yourself why. Maybe it shields you from fear or allows you to avoid the uncomfortable fact that you don't know what you want. Or lets you say you're too busy, and have no time.

Whatever it is, get to the real reason you're not moving forward and look for my advice in the appropriate chapters of this book.

Some Final Thoughts

Living a life you love – like anything that involves change – might not be an easy undertaking. However I hope that this book has helped you, and that you now feel more inspired, motivated and confident about building a happy life.

The need to change might come up with most urgency for you when you're at a crossroads, or have come to a point where you hate the life you're living. Yet in some ways change is an ongoing task. It's about continually adjusting your life to who you are, as you grow and change.

So keep this book at your side to guide and support you.

And remember: Your change can be as big or as small as you need it to be. Whether it's a sweeping life transformation or well-placed tweak – every change is good if it makes life better for you.

* It doesn't matter where you start – only that you do start. So pick one area, one issue to address, and one thing you can do. Pick something easy if you're scared, something quick if you're busy. But start!
* Changing your life *can* fit into your schedule. Break it down into small, simple steps. Take one step at a time. Little, often and regular will take you a long way!
* 'Mistakes' and 'failing' are part of the package.

Don't get too hung up on them. Consider it all as experience, ask yourself what you can learn, and do it differently as you progress!

- Don't forget to enjoy the ride! Changing your life for the better is exciting, energising and motivating. It's a voyage of discovery – so how about making the most of the new experiences it brings?

Change can be hard work. But you'll find that it's also rewarding and worthwhile.

Of course, there are times for change, and times for consolidation, too. We cannot always be ripping things out, moving them about, trying the new and the different – we also need to give ourselves some breaks. Remember to enjoy and savour life after every change. Breathe. Rest. Let things sink in. Just be for a while.

Because more change will inevitably happen – whether you initiate it, or whether it hits you, unwanted, out of the blue. And my hope is that this book will then be there for you again, as your companion and resource, to help you tackle and overcome the obstacles that you might encounter on the way – and yes, the excuses, too.

To the wonderful life *you* love!

About the Author

Monica Castenetto is a life coach, workshop leader, writer and speaker on personal change and Living a Life You Love. She helps people at life's crossroads to find out what's next, and to create happier, fuller lives for themselves.

Her other passions include her family, nurturing local entrepreneurs, and singing and performing gospel music.

Monica is an Italian, born and bred in Switzerland, and has been living in London for 17 years.

Acknowledgements

My warmest and most appreciative thanks go to:

All those who have generously contributed their excuses – you know who you are!

My beautiful clients who have allowed me to use their stories in this book.

Julian Gill, for painstaking proofreading.

My dear friends Jane Inglese, Regina Gill, and Clair Battaglino. and my sister Cinzia Castenetto, for listening to my ideas for this book, as well as test-reading it, and letting me have their thoughtful feedback and refining ideas.

My mother, Marina Castenetto Pelizzari, for always believing in me.

My publisher Joanne Henson for giving me this wonderful opportunity and providing the structure, integrity and guidance for the writing of this book.

Reference /
Bibliography

Richard Bach, Illusions: The Adventures of a Reluctant Messiah
Dell Publishing Co, 1977

Ann Brashares, The Sisterhood of the Travelling Pants
Delacorte Press, 2001

Brene Brown
http://brenebrown.com/2015/06/18/own-our-history-change-the-story/

Joseph Campbell
http://academyofideas.com/2013/12/joseph-campbell-other-people-have-a-lot-of-plans-for-you/

Stephanie Dowrick, Choosing Happiness
Allen & Unwin Australia, 1 Jan 2005

Wayne Dyer
http://www.brainyquote.com/quotes/quotes/w/wayne-dyer173497.html

Sue Fitzmaurice
https://www.facebook.com/SueFitzmauriceAuthor

Joline Godfrey
http://www.supercoach.com/tvdetail.php?recordID=142

T H Holmes & R H Rahe, The Social Readjustment Rating Scale
Journal of Psychosomatic Research, 11,213, 1967

Phillippa Lally, Cornelia H M van Jaarsveld, Henry W W Potts & Jane Wardle, How are habits formed: Modelling habit formation in the real world
European Journal of Social Psychology, 2010

Abraham Maslow, The Hierarchy of Needs – A Theory of Human Motivation
Psychological review, 1943

Caroline Myss
http://addictquotes.blogspot.co.uk/2010/08/empowering-quotes-by-caroline-myss.html

Badia P, McBane B & Suter S, Preference behavior in an immediate versus variably delayed shock situation with and without a warning signal
Journal of Experimental Psychology, Vol 72(6), Dec 1966, 847-852

Abigail A Mengers, The Benefits of Being Yourself: An Examination of Authenticity, Uniqueness, and Well-Being
http://repository.upenn.edu/mapp_capstone/63

Kevin Ngo, Let's Do This: 100 Motivational Messages to Inspire Action
CreateSpace, 2013

James O Prochaska, John C Norcross, Carlo C DiClemente, Changing for Good
Harper Collins, 1994

Mary Anne Radmacher, Courage Doesn't Always Roar
Conari Press, 2009

Robin Sharma
http://www.robinsharma.com/blog/10/my-20-best-quotes-for-high-achievement/

Norman Vincent Peale, Enthusiasm Makes the Difference
First Fireside, 2003

Joss Whedon
http://news.impossible.com/joss-whedon-the-man-
who-brought-you-buzz-and-buffy-giving-you-free-
screenwriting-class/

Marianne Williamson, A Return to Love
Harper Collins, 1992

Index

Also in this series

What's Your Excuse for not Eating Healthily?

Joanne Henson
Overcome your excuses and eat well to look good and feel great

Do you wish you could eat more healthily and improve the way you look and feel, but find that all too often life gets in the way? Do you regularly embark on healthy eating plans or diets but find that you just can't stick with them? Then this is the book for you.

This isn't another diet book. Instead it's a look at the things which have tripped you up in the past and offers advice, ideas and inspiration to help you overcome those things this time around.

No willpower? Hate healthy food? Got no time to cook? Crave sugary snacks? Overcome all of these excuses and many more. Change your eating habits and relationship with food *for good*.

"Very useful, very practical and makes a lot of sense!

There are some great tips in here and even if you just implemented a bit of Joanne's advice it would make a real difference"

Chantal Cooke, journalist & broadcaster

Paperback – ISBN 978-0-9933388-2-3
e-book – ISBN 978-0-9933388-3-0

Also in this series

What's Your Excuse for not Getting Fit?

Joanne Henson
Overcome your excuses and get active, healthy and happy

Do you want to be fit, lean and healthy, but find that all too often life gets in the way? Do you own a gym membership you don't use, or take up running every January only to give up in February? Then this is the book for you.

This is not yet another get-fit-quick program. It's a look at the things which have prevented you in the past from becoming the fit, active person you've always wanted to be, and a source of advice, inspiration and ideas to help you overcome those things this time around. Change your habits and attitude to exercise for good.

Too tired? Lacking motivation? Bored by exercise? You won't be after reading this book!

"Joanne is a true inspiration! Her passion, commitment

*and no nonsense attitude never fails to motivate her
clients to get moving and achieve their health and
fitness goals"*

Sarah Price, triathlete and five times Ironman finisher

Paperback – ISBN 978-0-9933388-0-9
e-book – ISBN 978-0-9933388-1-6